LOVE VEGAN

• •

The Essential Asian Cookbook for Vegans

Zoe Hazan

LOVE VEGAN

The Essential Asian Cookbook for Vegans

High Cedar Press

Copyright © 2020

Paperback Edition

All rights reserved. No part of this publication may be reproduced, distributed, stored in a retrieval system or transmitted in any form or by any means, including photocopying, recording, or other electronic or mechanical methods, without the prior written permission of the publisher.

The right of High Cedar Press to be identified as the authors of the work has been asserted in accordance with the Copyright, Designs and Patents Act 1988.

Published by High Cedar Press

Illustrations Copyright © 2020

DISCLAIMER

The full contents of 'Love Vegan', including text, comments, graphics, images, and other content are for informational purposes only. The information is not intended to diagnose, treat, cure or prevent any illnesses or diseases. Always consult you physician before changing dietary habits.

'Love Vegan' does not provide specific information or advice regarding food intolerance or allergies. It is the responsibility of the reader to ensure any diagnosed or potential food intolerances are identified and excluded from the recipes.

The author and publisher make no guarantee as to the availability of ingredients mentioned in this book. Many ingredients vary in size and texture and these differences may affect the outcome of some recipes. The author has tried to make the recipes as accurate and workable as possible, however cannot be responsible for any recipe not working.

Every effort has been made to prepare this material to ensure it's accuracy, however the author nor publisher will be held responsible if there is information deemed as inaccurate.

CONTENTS

Asian Favorites Made Easy — 7
Veganism in a Nutshell — 8
Plant Based Power — 11
Nourish Yourself — 13
Asian Fusion — 15
Equipment — 16
Pantry Staples — 17
Love Vegan — 18

MAINS

Perfect Pad Thai — 20
Take Out Style Chow Mein — 22
Singapore Fried Noodles — 24
Sweet & Sour Vegetable Stir-Fry — 26
Vegetable Lo Mein — 28
Kaeng Phanaeng Neua (Panang Curry) — 30
Creamy Thai Massaman Curry — 32
Authentic Thai Green Curry — 34
Spicy Thai Pizza with Peanut Satay Sauce — 36
General Tso's Cauliflower — 39
Kung Pao Chickpeas — 41
Sticky Chili Garlic Tofu — 43
Teriyaki Sweet Potato with Fluffy Cauliflower Rice — 45
Vietnamese Fresh Summer Rolls — 47
Tofu Skewers with Satay Sauce — 49
Crunchy Cashew Coconut Rice with Ginger Peanut Drizzle — 51
Quinoa, Avocado & Spinach Sushi Rolls — 53
Spicy Sichuan Eggplant — 55
Malaysian Laksa — 57
Vietnamese Pho — 59
Quick & Easy Miso Soup — 61
Gyoza (Japanese Dumplings) — 62

CONTENTS

SIDES

Nasu Dengaku (Miso Glazed Eggplant)	65
Chinese Special Fried Rice	67
Japanese Tempura	69
Tod Man Khao Pod (Thai Corn Fritters)	71
Crunchy Asian Salad with Sweet Sesame Vinaigrette	73
Chili Garlic Mushrooms	75
Sautéed Broccoli with Asian Garlic Sauce	76
Soft Chinese Bao Buns	77
Coconut & Lime Rice	80
Coconut Crusted Tofu Bites with Creamy Thai Green Sauce	81

DESSERTS

Coconut Matcha Tarts	84
Jian Dui (Fried Sesame Balls)	87
Coconut Sticky Rice with Mango	89
Crispy Banana Fritters with Sesame Seeds	91
Hup Tul Woo (Chinese Sweet Walnut Soup)	93
Ginger-Infused Japanese Rice Pudding	95
Black Sesame Seed Ice Cream	97
Sweet Thai Coconut Pancakes	100

EXTRAS

Sweet Chili Dipping Sauce	102
Vegan Oyster Sauce	103
Peanut Satay Sauce	104
Spinach and Sesame Crackers	105
Edamame Pâté	107
Thai Mango-Coconut Bubble Tea	108

LOVE VEGAN THE ULTIMATE ASIAN COOKBOOK FOR VEGANS

ASIAN FAVORITES MADE EASY

From sweet & sour stir-fries and creamy Massaman curries, to Vietnamese fresh summer rolls and Chinese Bao buns, this cookbook celebrates the flavors of the East and shows you how easy it is to prepare exotic and delicious vegan dishes in your very own kitchen - even on the busiest of weeknights.

The Essential Asian Cookbook for Vegans combines exotic cuisine from Thailand to Malaysia to Japan, and proves that even the most inexperienced chef can easily recreate authentic dishes at home. Each recipe has been tried, tested and refined to retain the delicate flavors of the East with a few tweaks to make it suitable for the vegan diet.

The Love Vegan cookbook series follows the philosophy that delicious, exciting and authentically flavored food can be created using simple and easy to find ingredients. Weeknight meals should not take longer than 30 minutes to prepare, providing you and your family with dishes that can rival any take-out.

This cookbook series aims to shed some light on the vegan lifestyle and health benefits that follow. We believe that whatever your reasons are for integrating vegan food into your diet the end result should be full of flavor and authenticity. Whether you are a vegan, a vegetarian or a meat-eater looking to reduce the amount of meat based meals in your diet, this book can help inspire you to cook delicious dishes every night of the week.

So what are you waiting for, start your Asian vegan journey today!

VEGANISM IN A NUTSHELL

Veganism is often viewed as a radical dietary way of life, yet more and more people are moving towards eating less meat and more plant-based food. The need to live a healthy lifestyle in today's world is self-evident. More than ever before we are faced with increased stress that undermines our body's immune systems, not to mention the many chemicals, hormones and pollutants we are subjected to through our food intake. It, therefore, makes sense to increase the quantity of natural and easily digestible foods in our diet to give our body the best chance we can of being healthier.

The average meat-eater consumes three times the amount of protein daily than their bodies need. You can get the necessary daily protein from a few delicious Quinoa, Avocado and Spinach Sushi Rolls. Add a slither of pickled ginger and a pinch of wasabi and you have covered your protein, omega oil and iron intake for the day. Ginger gives you a great digestive and immune system boost and wasabi is full of anti-cancer benefits as well as awakening your taste buds with its sharp bite. What a healthy and delicious alternative to an oily burger and fries!

Why add vegan food to your diet? Western civilisation consumes a lot more meat than Eastern civilisations, and we are far less healthy for it. Growth hormones in milk and meat are added to increase the growth cycle, and once eaten, these hormones and unnatural substances are transferred to your body and carry on their work. This creates many unwanted medical illnesses such as premature puberty, asthma and digestive disorders - all of which can be avoided by following a better eating plan. All it takes is simply adding more vegetables, whole grains and pulses to your diet, and this cookbook can help by inspiring you to cook creative and exciting recipes. The more natural ingredients you eat, the more you are working towards a better and healthier you.

So what is a vegan? There is a difference in the diet of vegetarians and vegans. True veganism is a dietary lifestyle where no animal products are consumed at all. It is not only about the food they eat but also the environmental impact and the desire to reduce the pressure on the earth's resources.

Vegans are conscious of the carbon footprint of the food they consume. They strive to ensure the impact is as minimal as possible and their food does not have to be transported halfway around the world to land on their plate. Although true veganism is eliminating all animal products from your diet, we believe you should do what works for you.

Vegetarians, on the other hand will not consume any meat, but they will eat animal produce such as eggs, cheese and milk. As there are so many hidden animal products in food, a vegan or vegetarian has to be very careful with what they eat. Should you want to go meat-free be sure to read the ingredients on products, do a bit of research and always ask questions in restaurants. You'd be surprised to find that many a vegetable soup has been made with chicken stock!

So many people shun veganism because they don't believe a pure plant based diet can satisfy their taste buds, but this couldn't be further from the truth. They have this image of vegans either being Buddhist monks or hippies. Whilst both of these are lifestyle choices and both have very sound principles, they may not be the way for you to go. Our grandmothers with their grey broccoli that used to leave a watery mess on our plates are a far cry from a fresh, crisp stir-fry or a tasty Pad Thai that you will find in this cookbook. Veganism is thinking outside of the box, it is a different way of looking at food and at life. This book will throw that image of grey broccoli out of the window forever and prove that authentic mouthwatering food can be available for the vegan diet too.

Most of us can attest to being thoroughly disappointed by recipes that claim to be purely vegan, only for them to feature some 'hidden' animal products or taste like raw tofu. Each recipe in this book has been carefully tried, tested and refined to retain an authentic flavor and best of all, each recipe is not only suitable for vegans but also for people who desires to make their eating habits healthier and tastier.

You can substitute the herbs, spices or any other ingredients used in our recipes to add your signature touch. The important thing to remember is that the greatest chefs cook with their heart. They experiment with food. Be daring, be creative and use these recipes as a base for making new recipes of your own. Use them as a springboard into a new and exciting world of vegan cooking and you won't be disappointed.

PLANT BASED POWER

'You are what you eat'

The increasing popularity of the vegan diet is linked to a growing number of significant and well-documented health benefits. In recent times, the media has shed some light on the vegan lifestyle and quashed any myths that a vegan diet cannot sufficiently source all the nutrients we need to live a healthy and balanced life. There is plenty of science to support a plant based diet but personal transformations such as curing diabetes, overcoming obesity and leading a more active and energized life seem to make the biggest impression.

Whether you decide to make one day a week a meatless day or whether you decide to fully adopt a vegan lifestyle you will feel better, have more energy and be more resistant to illness. It is important to keep in mind that what you put into your body should be working with your body, not against it. It is the same concept as running uphill as opposed to running along a flat path. More energy is expended by digesting meat and processed food than by eating easily digestible and nutritious vegetables and pulses.

You should always try to avoid any genetically modified foods. Eating something that has been modified in a laboratory to be resistant to being dissolved by nature is going to give your body's digestive enzymes a hard time trying to break it down as it has been modified to withstand exactly that. Eat with your head and try to think about what you are putting into your body.

One of the most prevalent assumptions about veganism is that you need animal products to source important nutrients, vitamins and minerals in order to live a healthy and balanced life. Take a look at the below information for an indication of how a plant-based diet can sufficiently provide you with everything your body needs, without animal produce.

Protein: Nuts, seeds, cereals, grains, beans, and soy (tofu or other soy based products)

Calcium: Dark leafy greens, nuts and seeds, fresh and dried fruits and whole wheat bread

Iron: Leafy greens, wholemeal bread, grains, tofu/tempeh, lentils, and legumes

Potassium: White beans, potatoes (including the skin), apricots, yogurt, bananas

Magnesium: Leafy greens, pumpkin seeds, brown rice, dark chocolate

Vitamin C: Citrus, yellow bell peppers, kiwis, broccoli, strawberries, tomatoes

Vitamin A: Sweet potato, carrots, lettuce, paprika, mangoes, kale, dried apricots

Adopting a vegan diet doesn't necessarily mean you're automatically healthier. Even if you're vegan you could technically live on sugar, Oreos, and french fries – so it's all a matter of how you do it.

This book will inspire you to cook exciting, delicious and flavorsome dishes while still following a healthy lifestyle and providing your body with nourishment. As an example, Chickpeas are good at keeping insulin levels stable, which means you won't get that sleepy feeling after eating. The Kung Pao Chickpea recipe in this book is a perfect lunch or dinner meal to keep you feeling full without that glucose dip that you often get after a big meal. The Vegetable Lo Mein is packed with leafy greens, helping you get your recommended daily allowance of iron, potassium, and calcium.

For those with a sweet tooth, this recipe book has some really tasty sweet treats such as Coconut Sticky Rice with Mango, Crispy Banana Fritters with Sesame Seeds or Ginger-infused Japanese Rice Pudding.

NOURISH YOURSELF

Asian food best combines nutrients from vegetables, pulses, and legumes with the medicinal qualities of herbs and spices to create meals that optimize the ingredients for healthy eating.

Let's take a look at a few common Asian spices and their health benefits:

Chilies

Naturally high in vitamin C and a good source of Vitamin A and E. They act as a blood purifier and are great for aiding digestion as well as helping to relieve migraines and aching muscles and joints.

Turmeric

A powerful antioxidant which also helps ward off dementia and reduce the risk of cancer. It also produces a wonderfully warm golden color when added to curries.

Ginger

Aids good digestion and helps eliminate that bloated feeling after meals. Fresh ginger root is best as it can be grated and fried with your onions and adds a delicious lemony aroma and flavor to curries.

Cinnamon

Excellent at regulating blood sugar levels as well as reducing heart disease and lowering cholesterol.

Cardamom, Coriander, and Cumin

All help oxygenate your blood and add a huge flavorsome punch to Asian dishes.

Garlic

A natural antibiotic as well as adding a deep level of flavor to food.

Coconut Milk

Widely used as a base for curries, coconut milk is a great source of magnesium and can help aid the immune system and promote weight loss. People who are allergic to tree nuts should always ask if a curry has coconut milk in it, as it can cause an allergic reaction.

Soy Sauce

This is a staple in Japanese food and brings out a salty, nutty and earthy flavor. You can get light soy that is used with sushi and dark soy that is used for cooking. The dark soy has a wonderful salty caramel flavor that enhances most foods.

Mint

Great at aiding digestion as well as helping to alleviate symptoms of IBS. The herb is a wonderful way to cool your mouth when eating a hot curry and also makes a delicious base for a dipping sauce with raw veggies.

Coriander

Dried cilantro spice or cilantro leaves are used in curries as it has a superb earthy taste. It is a great source of dietary fiber as well as magnesium and vitamin C. The leaves of the fresh plant are known as Dhania and add an fresh and crisp flavor to curry. They can be put on top as a garnish and also eaten with the curry.

Lemon Grass

Commonly used to treat stomach aches and high blood pressure, lemon grass is great at killing germs so can be used to treat the common cold. It smells summery and adds a freshness to all Asian food, especially curries.

ASIAN FUSION

From eye-catching Sushi Rolls to warm and comforting Miso soup, you are sure to find something to tempt your taste buds in this cookbook. The recipes in this book are easy to prepare using everyday ingredients that you will find at your local supermarket.

Asian food is characterized by its place of origin. The culture of an Asian region is what determines the foods eaten in that area. For example, Japan is well known for fermented soy products and rice and the Japanese gastronomy is where sushi originates from. A common misnomer is that vegans can't eat sushi. If you eliminate the fish and use a vegan mayonnaise substitute you have a delicious, fresh and wonderfully healthy meal. You could use the recipe in this book to make your own sushi – that way you know exactly what goes into it. It will give you great respect for the Sushi master at your local sushi restaurant!

The aim of this recipe book is to make eating healthier much easier so that it can be incorporated into your daily diet, and most of these recipes take no longer than 30 minutes to prepare. The ingredients used in this cookbook are straightforward, basic ingredients. We've all been frustrated by recipes that call for a very specific special item that takes days to source and then remains in your cupboard until it exceeds the expiry date and you have to throw it in the bin. By making sure that all the ingredients are easy to find, you will be able to source them quickly and use them more often. You will also be able to adapt the recipes as you get more adventurous and excited at how great your eating change is making you feel.

Eating out in restaurants can be a trying experience for a vegan. That is one of the great benefits of cooking Asian food at home. For the Eastern palate understands that meat is just one ingredient of a wide choice of many. There are so many different tastes and flavors on offer, and this book combines the most popular and classic dishes, making it the only vegan cookbook series you will need.

EQUIPMENT

WOK

The wok is by far the most important utensil when cooking Asian cuisine. It is made from heavy iron or steel and great when you need to whip up a quick dinner. This concave shaped pan is very versatile and perfect for stir-frying, stewing or deep frying.

You can find a good quality wok at most supermarkets, and always buy one with a nice solid base so that the heat is evenly distributed. Watch the food cooking in a wok closely as it cooks faster than conventional methods.

STEAMER

This is used for steaming rice, vegetables, buns, dumplings and to make dim sum. It is a very handy yet inexpensive piece of equipment and is sure to be used frequently when cooking Asian food. A bamboo steamer is the most traditional type of steamer and has the additional benefit of steaming more than one layer of food simultaneously.

SUSHI MAT

The most simple, easy and foolproof method of making sushi is with a bamboo sushi mat. For a newbie, making sushi can be very frustrating and not to mention a messy affair. If you enjoy sushi and are likely to make it a few times for yourself, your family or your friends it is worth investing in a sushi mat.

BAMBOO SKEWERS

Great for grilling vegetables and tofu. Most commonly used when vegetables or tofu have been marinated or flavored, grilled and then served with satay sauce or sweet chili dipping sauce. Be sure to soak the skewers in water for around 10 minutes before skewering the tofu or veggies to prevent them from burning.

PANTRY STAPLES

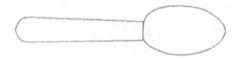

To make your life easier and to ensure your kitchen is equipt with staple items most commonly used in Asian cooking it is advisable that you have a well-stocked pantry to avoid a last minute trip to the supermarket after a long day at work.

The list below is a variety of simple and straightforward ingredients that you should keep in your cupboards, ready to whip up a delicious exotic Asian dish at any time.

The 'F' symbol means this can be frozen, reducing the amount of waste and by keeping a well-stocked freezer you can ensure you have these ingredients to hand at all times. For best results, you may need to check the most suitable method of freezing for the following items.

Chilies (F)
Fresh ginger (F)
Fresh garlic (F)
Lemongrass (F)
Fresh cilantro (F)
Rice vinegar
Sesame Oil
Cumin
Canned coconut milk
Peanut butter
Soy sauce
Dry or canned beans – any variety
Noodles
Rice
Nuts

LOVE VEGAN

We love Asian food because of the delicate combination of aromatic flavors that make your taste buds sing.

This cookbook is focused on basic, natural and wholesome ingredients, and when cooked in the right way and perfectly flavored you can create beautiful, exotic and mouth-watering vegan dishes, regardless of your cooking ability.

Whether you are a long term follower of the vegan lifestyle, a beginner in need of an easy way to get started or a meat-eater looking to incorporate meat-free Mondays into your week, this book will give you some deliciously authentic recipes for any occasion.

So get ready for some exotic and easy to cook vegan meals that will open up a whole new world for you.

MAINS

PERFECT PAD THAI

Pad Thai originates from Thailand and is commonly served as street food. This incredibly simple and easy dish is bursting with authentic flavors.

Preparation Time
20 minutes

Total Time
30 minutes

Makes
6 servings

INGREDIENTS

FOR THE PAD THAI

8oz / 230g package rice noodles
3 tbsp sesame oil
3 garlic cloves, minced
1 tsp ginger, minced
¼ cup soy sauce
2 tbsp rice wine vinegar (you can substitute for white vinegar)
¼ cup brown sugar
1 tbsp paprika
½ cup cubed extra firm tofu, pressed and drained
1 tsp hoisin sauce (can be substituted for 1 tsp soy sauce)
3 scallions, chopped plus ½ cup for garnish
1 cup bean sprouts, plus ½ cup for garnish
¼ cup unsalted peanuts, lightly roasted and crushed
½ lime, cut into wedges, for garnish

FOR THE PEANUT SAUCE

½ - 1 tbsp red chili paste (depending on how spicy you like it)
1 cup coconut milk
1 tbsp soy sauce
½ cup peanut butter
1 tbsp brown sugar

DIRECTIONS

In a medium sized bowl soak the rice noodle for 30 minutes then drain and set aside.

While the noodles are soaking make the peanut sauce by combining all sauce ingredients in a small saucepan and slowly bring to a boil. Reduce and cook for 2-3 minutes until the sauce thickens. Remove from the heat and set aside.

Heat a large frying pan or wok over medium-high heat and stir-fry ginger and garlic for 2-3 minutes. Reduce heat to medium-low and add the noodles, stir-frying for 2 minutes until they have softened.

Add the soy sauce, sugar, vinegar and paprika, stirring constantly.

Stir in the tofu and mix well to combine all ingredients, cooking for about 2-3 minutes. Add hoisin sauce, scallions, ground peanuts and bean sprouts, and continuously stir to prevent ingredients from sticking to the bottom of the pan. Stir-fry for a further 3 minutes. Add a dash of water if the dish appears to be too dry.

Remove from the heat and garnish with scallions, bean sprouts, and a lime wedge and pour peanut sauce over the top.

TAKE OUT STYLE CHOW MEIN

The wonderful combination of soft noodles and crunchy vegetables make this popular dish a real crowd pleaser. With only 5 minutes preparation time, this meal can be on the dinner table in 15 minutes, making it an ideal dish for busy weeknights.

Preparation Time
5 minutes

Total Time
15 minutes

Makes
4 servings

INGREDIENTS

7oz / 200g noodles
2 tbsp sesame or vegetable oil
½ onion, finely chopped
3 garlic cloves, minced
1-2 red chili (deseeded), thinly sliced
5.2oz / 150g mushrooms, thinly sliced

3.5oz / 100g snap peas
3.5oz / 100g bean sprouts
5 tbsp soy sauce
2 tbsp rice vinegar
1 tbsp brown sugar
4 scallions, chopped

DIRECTIONS

Bring a medium sized saucepan filled with water to the boil and cook noodles according to packet directions, usually no more than 5-6 minutes. Once cooked, drain and discard water.

While the noodles are cooking heat a large wok with oil over medium heat, and once hot add the onions, garlic, and chili. Saute for 2-3 minutes, add mushrooms, peas and bean sprouts then stir-fry for 4-5 minutes. Stir frequently to prevent the vegetables from sticking to the bottom.

Add the noodles to the stir-fry, then add in soy sauce, rice vinegar, and brown sugar, mixing well to combine. Cook for another 2-3 minutes and serve immediately while hot. Garnish with scallions.

SINGAPORE FRIED NOODLES

This healthy Asian stir-fry is low in calories and packed full of flavor. It is recommended you chop and prepare all of the ingredients beforehand as you will need to work fast when stir-frying.

Preparation Time
10 minutes

Total Time
25 minutes

Makes
4 servings

INGREDIENTS

2 tbsp sesame or vegetable oil
1-inch fresh ginger, grated
4 garlic cloves, minced
½ onion, thinly sliced
1 medium carrot, peeled and thinly sliced diagonally
½ red bell pepper, de-seeded and thinly sliced
½ green bell pepper, de-seeded and thinly sliced
½ cup bean sprouts
½ head broccoli, cut into small florets then halved
8.8oz / 250g vermicelli rice noodles
2 tbsp yellow curry powder
½ tsp dried chili flakes or crushed red pepper flakes
1 ½ tbsp soy sauce
½ cup coconut milk
2 tbsp cilantro, chopped
¼ cup unsalted peanuts, crushed (optional)

DIRECTIONS

Soak noodles in a bowl of warm water for 15-20 minutes or prepare according to packet directions. Drain well once cooked.

While noodles are soaking heat a large wok or pan with oil over medium-high heat, then add garlic and ginger. Saute for 1 minute then add curry powder and remaining vegetables, stirring frequently.

Stir-fry for 5 minutes or until the vegetables begin to soften then add soy sauce, chili flakes, and noodles. Cook for a further minute then add the coconut milk, ensuring all ingredients are well combined.

Remove from the heat and serve immediately.

SWEET & SOUR VEGETABLE STIR-FRY

This recipe combines tangy and sweet flavors for an authentic homemade sauce that could rival any take-out. It's packed full of vegetables and is a quick and convenient dish to whip up for the whole family.

Preparation Time
10 minutes

Total Time
20 minutes

Makes
4 servings

INGREDIENTS

3.5oz / 100g bok choy, sliced lengthwise
1 cup cauliflower, chopped into small pieces
1 carrot, thinly sliced
¾ cup snap peas
1 tomato, chopped
½ onion, finely chopped
3 garlic cloves, minced

3 tbsp tomato sauce
2 tbsp soy sauce
1 tbsp brown sugar
1 cup vegetable stock
2 tsp cornstarch
1 tbsp sesame or vegetable oil
Rice or noodles to serve

DIRECTIONS

Heat oil in a wok or pan over medium-high heat. Once hot add onions and saute for 2-3 minutes, then add garlic and fry for a further minute.

Add bok choy, cauliflower, carrot, tomato and peas and stir-fry for 1-2 minutes, moving the vegetables around constantly to evenly cook and prevent them from sticking to the bottom of the pan.

Add tomato sauce, soy sauce and brown sugar, and stir-fry for a minute to allow the flavors to intensify. Pour in 1 cup of vegetable stock and bring to a boil then reduce to a simmer.

Add cornstarch to a small bowl and whisk with 1 tbsp water to dissolve the starch and form a thick paste.

Pour into the wok and cook for 5-7 minutes until the sauce thickens.

Serve immediately while hot over freshly cooked rice or noodles.

VEGETABLE LO MEIN

This simple yet versatile dish is full of vegetables and is healthy and easy to make. Be sure to drain your noodles well before adding them as wet noodles will make your stir-fry soggy.

Preparation Time
5 minutes

Total Time
15 minutes

Makes
4-5 servings

INGREDIENTS

FOR THE NOODLES

2 tbsp olive oil
1 lb / 450g rice noodles
1 red pepper, chopped
1 yellow pepper, chopped
Handful of Chinese greens (Bok Choy, Choy Sum etc)
1 large onion, chopped
2 tbsp fresh ginger, grated
2 garlic cloves, minced
2-3 scallions, cut diagonally
1 cup fresh cilantro or Thai basil, chopped

FOR THE SAUCE

¼ cup brown sugar
2 tbsp tomato puree
1 cup vegetable stock
4 tsp cornstarch
2 tbsp sesame oil
⅓ cup soy sauce
¼ cup rice wine vinegar

DIRECTIONS

In a small bowl whisk together the sauce ingredients until well combined and set aside.

Bring a saucepan of water to a boil and cook noodles according to packet directions.

While noodles are cooking heat a large wok or skillet over medium-high heat and stir-fry the onions, ginger, and garlic for 30 seconds, then add the peppers and cook for a further

3-4 minutes until tender. Add the noodles, Chinese greens, and scallions.

Pour in sauce and heat for 1-2 minutes, mixing well to ensure all ingredients are coated.

Add fresh herbs then remove from the heat and serve immediately.

KAENG PHANAENG NEUA (PANANG CURRY)

This popular curry originates from Malaysia but can be found in many regions around South East Asia. The sauce is rich and creamy, with a sweet aromatic flavor and a hint of chili.

Preparation Time
15 minutes

Total Time
30 minutes

Makes
4 servings

INGREDIENTS

2 tbsp sesame or vegetable oil
3 cloves garlic, chopped
1 tsp ginger, grated
3 tbsp vegan Panang curry paste (can be found in the International section at a large supermarket)
2 cans (14.1oz / 400g) coconut milk
1 tbsp brown sugar
2 tbsp soy sauce
1 ½ tbsp freshly squeezed lime juice
¼ cup unsalted cashew nuts, lightly roasted and chopped
1 cup onion, chopped
4 Thai basil leaves or a handful of cilantro, chopped (plus a little more to garnish)
5.2oz / 150g extra firm tofu, cubed
½ head broccoli, cut into small florets
1 cup red bell peppers, thinly sliced
1 cup mushrooms, chopped (you can use any variety you like)
½ cup snap peas

DIRECTIONS

To start, remove tofu from packaging and press between two towels to remove excess water. You can use something weighted, such as a large saucepan or chopping board and place this on top of the tofu to squeeze out as much moisture as possible for a minimum of 10 minutes. This process will allow the tofu to absorb much more flavor. After 10 minutes chop tofu into small cubes.

In a large wok or pan heat oil over medium-high heat. Add onions and saute for 2-3 minutes until soft. Add ginger and garlic and cook for 1-2 minutes. Stir in curry paste and heat for 1 minute to allow it to soften.

Pour in coconut milk, soy sauce, brown sugar and lime juice and mix well to combine.

Add the broccoli, pepper, mushroom, tofu, and fresh herbs and cook on a low simmer for 10-15 minutes until the veggies and tofu and cooked throughout and the sauce has thickened.

While the curry is cooking make the rice according to the packet directions.

Serve hot over rice and garnish with cashew nuts and fresh herbs.

CREAMY THAI MASSAMAN CURRY

Massaman curry is infused with exotic Thai flavors and combines a beautifully rich and creamy sauce with sweet and nutty flavors. Although this curry uses many ingredients there are very few stages, making it a quick and easy meal to prepare.

Preparation Time
10 minutes

Total Time
25 minutes

Makes
4 servings

INGREDIENTS

2 tbsp coconut or sesame oil
½ cup onion, finely chopped
2 tsp fresh ginger, grated
4 garlic cloves, minced
½ head cauliflower, chopped into small florets
1 red bell pepper, thinly sliced
1 cup green beans, chopped
¾ cup carrots, thinly sliced diagonally
3 tbsp red curry paste or massaman curry paste
1 tsp ground cumin powder
¼ tsp ground cinnamon powder
¼ tsp cardamom powder
½ tsp cloves powder
¼ tsp cayenne pepper
¼ tsp ground star anise
3 heaped tbsp peanut butter
1 tbsp brown sugar
½ tsp coarse salt
1 ½ tbsp soy sauce
2 cups canned coconut milk
1 cup vegetable stock
1 tbsp freshly squeezed lime juice
2 tbsp cilantro, chopped
Cooked white rice, to serve

DIRECTIONS

In a large saucepan heat oil over medium-high heat then saute onions for 2-3 minutes until soft. Add ginger and garlic and fry for 1 minute. Stir in carrot, cauliflower and beans and mix to combine. Partially cover the pan and cook for 4 minutes until the vegetables have softened a little.

Add red pepper, curry paste and all the spices. Fry for 2 minutes to soften the paste and roast the spices.

Mix in peanut butter, brown sugar, soy sauce, coconut milk, and vegetable stock and combine well. Cover pan and cook for 10 minutes, then uncover and cook for a further 3-4 minutes or until the sauce thickens.

Season and add chopped cilantro and lime juice.

Serve immediately over freshly cooked rice.

AUTHENTIC THAI GREEN CURRY

This popular dish is known for its sweet, fragrant and exotic flavors. There's nothing more authentic than making your own Thai Green Curry Paste and it will make a huge difference to the flavor of the curry. You can double the paste recipe and freeze it for up to a month.

Preparation Time
15 minutes

Total Time
30 minutes

Makes
3-4 servings

INGREDIENTS

FOR THE THAI GREEN CURRY PASTE

1 stalk fresh lemongrass, roughly chopped
1 tbsp ground cilantro
2 tsp ground cumin powder
2 tbsp soy sauce
1 tsp brown sugar
2 green chilies, thinly sliced
¼ cup red onion
3 garlic cloves, minced
1-inch fresh ginger, grated
1 tbsp freshly squeezed lime juice
3 tbsp fresh cilantro, chopped
½ tsp coarse salt
Up to ¼ cup coconut milk

FOR THE CURRY

1 can coconut milk
1 cup vegetable stock
1 tbsp soy sauce
1 tsp brown sugar
2 kaffir lime leaves
14oz / 400g medium-firm tofu, cut into cubes
1 small sweet potato, cut into small cubes
1 small zucchini, cut lengthwise then sliced
½ red bell pepper
Handful of fresh Thai basil or cilantro, chopped (optional)
2-3 tbsp vegetable or sesame oil for frying

DIRECTIONS

In a blender add all curry paste ingredients, except coconut milk, and pulse well until smooth. Add 1 tablespoon at a time of coconut milk to help the ingredients combine and form a smooth but thick paste.

In a large wok or pan heat oil over medium-high heat. Once hot add paste and stir-fry for 1-2 minutes until fragrant.

Pour in stock, coconut milk and kaffir lime leaves and bring to a boil, then reduce to a low simmer. Add sweet potatoes and tofu and simmer for 6-8 minutes until the sweet potato is tender when pierced with a fork. This will depend on how large or small the potato cubes are.

Add the zucchini and red pepper and cook for 5 minutes until the vegetables are tender but not mushy. Mix in soy sauce and sugar.

Remove from the heat, garnish with fresh basil and serve over freshly cooked rice.

SPICY THAI PIZZA WITH PEANUT SATAY SAUCE

A fail-proof recipe that proves how to easy it is to make both the pizza dough and sauce completely from scratch. The simple homemade satay topping really makes this pizza special and give it a sweet and nutty Thai flavor. The recipe is for 2 crusts so you can freeze one for another day.

Preparation Time
15 minutes
(+ 1 hour for the dough to rise)

Total Time
40 minutes

Makes
2 pizza crusts and enough sauce to top both pizzas / 1 Pizza can serve 2 people.

INGREDIENTS

FOR THE DOUGH

1 packet active dry yeast
1 tbsp white sugar
1 tbsp olive oil, plus more for brushing dough
1 tsp coarse salt
3 cups all-purpose flour
1 cup warm water (must be very warm when you poke your finger in but not uncomfortably hot)

FOR THE SAUCE

1 can full-fat coconut milk
2 tbsp vegan peanut butter
2 tbsp soy sauce
1 tbsp maple syrup
2 tsp freshly squeezed lime juice
1 tsp red wine vinegar
½ tsp dried chili flakes
¼ tsp coarse salt
¼ tsp freshly ground black pepper
2 tbsp cilantro, chopped

FOR THE TOPPINGS

1 tbsp sesame oil
1 cup red onion, thinly sliced
1 tbsp garlic, minced

1 tbsp ginger, minced
1 small red chili, deseeded and minced
7oz / 200g mushrooms, sliced
½ a red pepper, thinly sliced
8oz / 230g firm tofu, cut into small cubes
½ cup peanuts
Handful chopped cilantro, chopped

DIRECTIONS

In a small bowl add water and sprinkle over yeast. Leave to stand for 5 minutes until foam starts to appear on the surface.

After 5 minutes add sugar, oil and salt, and gently mix to combine, then transfer to the bowl of your stand mixer.

Using the dough hook slowly mix ingredients while adding flour, ½ a cup at a time, until a thick dough forms, around 4-5 minutes.

Scrape down the edges and pull all the dough in together. Drizzle a little olive into the bowl and coat all sides of the dough.

Cover with a kitchen towel and leave in a warm area for an hour.

After an hour the dough should have doubled in size. Cut in half using a knife and place both pieces on a lightly floured surface. Punch the dough to release air and gently knead for a minute or two. Roll one of the pieces into a 12-inch round pizza dough and lightly brush with olive oil. Set aside.

You can freeze the other piece for later use by placing in an airtight zip lock bag.

TO MAKE THE SAUCE:

Place all ingredients except cilantro in a small saucepan and cook over low heat, stirring occasionally. Cook for 20 minutes or until the sauce has thickened and reduced. Remove from heat and add chopped cilantro.

Preheat the oven to 220. Grease a baking tray with sesame oil.

While the sauce is cooking roast the tofu in the oven for 7-10 minutes until brown, turning the cubes after 5 minutes to ensure they cook evenly. Remove, but leave the oven on at 220°**c**.

In a large frying pan or wok heat sesame oil over medium heat. Stir-fry onions, garlic, ginger and chili for 3 minutes, stirring frequently. Add mushrooms and red pepper and cook for a further 3-4 minutes until all vegetables have softened but are not mushy.

Reduce heat to low then add half of the coconut sauce mixture and stir to combine. Heat the vegetables and sauce for 2-3 minutes.

Using a slotted spoon spread mixture over pizza dough, making sure to coat the entire surface but not adding too much sauce as your pizza will become soggy.

Top with peanuts and cilantro and bake for 12-15 minutes.

You can freeze any remaining sauce.

GENERAL TSO'S CAULIFLOWER

This mouthwatering dish combines sweet and spicy flavors with a sticky sauce that goes well with rice. This vegan version replaces chicken with cauliflower and is packed with vegetables, making this meal low calorie and healthy.

Preparation Time
15 minutes
(+ 15 minutes for cauliflower to marinate)

Total Time
30 minutes

Makes
4 servings

INGREDIENTS

FOR THE CAULIFLOWER

2 medium heads of cauliflower, cut into small florets
2 tbsp sesame oil
½ cup cornstarch
4 tbsp soy sauce Oil for frying (vegetable or sesame oil)

FOR THE SAUCE

2 tbs sesame oil
3 tsp fresh ginger, peeled & grated
4 garlic cloves, minced
2 cups vegetable stock
¼ cup light soy sauce
2 tbs corn flour
2 tsp chili sauce (you can use sriracha or garlic chili sauce found in the Asian section of a large supermarket)
¼ cup brown sugar, loosely packed
2 tbs vegetable or peanut oil
1 tsp rice wine vinegar
4 scallions, thinly sliced
White rice for serving

DIRECTIONS

To begin you need to marinate the cauliflower. In a large bowl whisk together soy sauce and sesame oil, then slowly add corn flour until a thick batter is formed. Add the cauliflower and mix until each floret is evenly coated. Leave to marinate for 15-20 minutes.

In a large frying pan or wok heat 2 tbsp of peanut or vegetable oil over medium-high heat.

Once the pan is hot add the cauliflower mixture in batches and cook until lightly browned on all sides. You do not want to overcrowd the pan so only fry a few at a time. Drizzle more oil on the pan if it appears to be sticking. Once crispy transfer to a plate lined with paper towels and set aside.

Using the same frying pan or wok saute ginger and garlic for 1 minute until fragrant, adding 1 tsp of oil if needed.

Add stock, soy sauce, corn flour, chili sauce, brown sugar, and rice wine vinegar and stir until fully combined. Slowly bring mixture to a boil then reduce to a simmer. Stir frequently while the sauce thickens.

Once the sauce has thickened and become glossy add the cauliflower and mix until each floret is coated with sauce.

Remove from heat, garnish with scallions and serve over white rice.

KUNG PAO CHICKPEAS

A Szechuan dish that is mildly spiced with sweet, sour and savory elements. The ingredients combine together to create an irresistible and delicious meal that's simple and convenient to make.

Preparation Time
15 minutes
(+ 15 minutes for cauliflower to marinate)

Total Time
30 minutes

Makes
4 servings

INGREDIENTS

FOR THE MARINADE

2 tbsp soy sauce
2 tbsp rice wine vinegar
1 lime, juiced and zested
1 tbsp maple syrup or brown sugar
1 tbsp coconut oil, melted
1 tbsp cornstarch

FOR THE CHICKPEAS

2 tbsp coconut oil
1 (14oz / 400g) can chickpeas, drained and rinsed
1 cup vegan kung pao sauce (found in the international section of a supermarket)
3 garlic cloves, minced
1-inch fresh ginger, grated
½ tsp dried chili flakes or red pepper flakes

FOR THE GARNISH

2 scallions, thinly sliced
1-2 Thai chili peppers or small red chilies, chopped
½ cup unsalted peanuts
2 tbsp fresh cilantro, chopped

Cooked white rice, for serving

DIRECTIONS

In a large bowl whisk together soy sauce, vinegar, lime, maple syrup, coconut oil and cornstarch until smooth. Add chickpeas and toss to combine. Cover the bowl and marinate in the fridge for a minimum of 30 minutes. The longer you are able to marinate the chickpeas for, the more flavor they will retain.

Heat coconut oil in a large pan or wok over medium-high heat. Add the ginger and garlic and saute for 1-2 minutes. Stir in the chickpeas along with the marinating sauce, kung pao sauce and chili flakes. Cook for around 8 minutes, stirring frequently.

Once cooked remove from heat, transfer to a serving bowl and garnish with cilantro, scallions and peanuts. Serve warm over freshly cooked white rice.

STICKY CHILI GARLIC TOFU

This simple dish is bursting with authentic Asian flavors. Pressing the tofu beforehand enables it to absorb much more flavor, and stir-frying it gives it a golden crisp coating.

Preparation Time
30 minutes
(including 10 minutes to press the tofu)

Total Time
45 minutes

Makes
4 servings

INGREDIENTS

1 lb / 450g extra firm tofu
1 ½ cups uncooked white or brown rice
4-5 scallions
4 tbsp sesame or vegetable oil, divided
1 tsp crushed red pepper flakes

1 tbsp sesame seeds (optional)
½ cup hoisin sauce
2 tbsp soy sauce
2-3 garlic cloves, minced

DIRECTIONS

To start, remove tofu from packaging and press between two towels to remove excess water. You can use something weighted, such as a large saucepan or a heavy chopping board and place this on top of the tofu to squeeze out as much moisture as possible for a minimum of 10 minutes. This process will allow the tofu to absorb much more flavor. After 10 minutes chop tofu into small cubes.

In a frying pan or wok add soy sauce, hoisin sauce, and garlic and stir until well combined. Add tofu and mix until each piece is thoroughly coated. Remove from the heat, and transfer to the fridge in a covered bowl for a minimum of 20 minutes.

Meanwhile, cook the rice according to packet directions then drain and cover with a towel once cooked. In a frying pan or wok heat 2 tablespoons of oil over medium heat. Add marinated tofu in a single layer along with the sauce and fry without stirring for 5 minutes. Flip each tofu cube and cook on the other side for 5 minutes. Add the scallions for the last 2 minutes of cooking.

Serve over warm rice and garnish with sesame seeds if using.

TERIYAKI SWEET POTATO WITH FLUFFY CAULIFLOWER RICE

Replacing white rice with cauliflower rice not only reduces the calories by almost half but makes for a very flavorsome meal as it is great at absorbing flavor. This Japanese inspired dish combines a sweet sticky sauce with hearty vegetables, making it a simple and healthy dinner for the whole family.

Preparation Time
15 minutes

Total Time
45 minutes

Makes
4 servings

INGREDIENTS

FOR THE CAULIFLOWER RICE

1 large head of cauliflower, leaves and large stems removed, roughly chopped
1 garlic clove, minced
½ inch ginger, grated

FOR THE TERIYAKI POTATO

2 medium sweet potatoes, cut into small wedges or cubes (skin on or off)
½ cup teriyaki sauce
2 tsp sriracha or chili sauce
1 tsp soy sauce
1 cup cooked edamame (optional)
1 cup corn kernels (canned or frozen)
1 ripe avocado, peeled, pitted and thinly sliced
3 scallions, sliced
1 tbsp sesame seeds, to garnish
extra teriyaki sauce, for serving (optional)

DIRECTIONS

Preheat the oven to 200°c. Grease a baking tray with a little oil and set aside.

In a large bowl add the cubed sweet potato and combine with teriyaki sauce, sriracha sauce and soy sauce. Toss to evenly coat and bake in the oven for 30-35 minutes, stirring occasionally. Remove from oven when the potatoes are tender when pierced with a fork, but not mushy.

While the potatoes are in the oven make the cauliflower rice. Add the cauliflower to a food processor and pulse in short bursts until the cauliflower resembles small grains of rice. Be careful not to over process this as you do not want a puree. If you do not have a food processor you can shred the cauliflower using a hand held grater.

Transfer cauliflower rice to a microwave-safe bowl and mix in ginger and garlic. Cover and microwave for 4-5 minutes, until rice is tender and cauliflower is cooked throughout. Set aside.

Once the sweet potatoes are cooked transfer to a large serving bowl and add scallions, corn, edamame, sesame seeds and avocado. Toss to combine and serve warm over cauliflower rice.

VIETNAMESE FRESH SUMMER ROLLS

These light, fresh and delicious rolls are a staple in Vietnam and a welcoming change from the deep fried versions that are more common. The rolls are great as an appetizer and surprisingly filling as a meal on its own. Rice paper wrappers are called 'Bahn Trang' and can be found in Asian supermarkets.

Preparation Time
10 minutes

Total Time
20 minutes

Makes
6 rolls

INGREDIENTS

2oz / 60g rice vermicelli
6 rice paper wrappers
A large bowl filled with water to dip rice paper sheets
Handful of cilantro leaves, roughly chopped
6-8 mint leaves, chopped
1 carrot, peeled and shredded

6 lettuce leaves
18 thinly sliced cucumber sticks
½ cup red cabbage, shredded
3 tbsp sesame seeds

DIRECTIONS

In a medium sized bowl soak noodles in boiling water for 3-4 minutes then drain and set aside.

In a separate bowl filled with warm water dip in rice paper sheets, one at a time, wetting all sides. Remove from water, shaking off any excess, and place in a single layer on a clean work surface or chopping board.

TO ASSEMBLE EACH ROLL:

Place a lettuce leaf, some rice noodles, a sprig of cilantro and mint, a little red cabbage, a tablespoon of grated carrots, 3 cucumber sticks and a sprinkle of sesame seeds. Do not overfill the rolls or they will be difficult to roll.

Take the bottom edge of the wrapper and tightly pull up over the filling. Fold the sides in over it. Continue to roll up tightly and transfer to a large plate, seam-side down. Repeat with remaining ingredients.

Serve with sweet chili or peanut dipping sauce.

The rolls can be served straight away or left in the fridge with a slightly damp cloth placed loosely over them to prevent them from drying out. Cover plate and damp cloth with a plastic wrap and refrigerate if you do not plan on serving them for at least half an hour.

TOFU SKEWERS WITH SATAY SAUCE

An easy recipe for crispy yet tender tofu covered in a sweet and creamy peanut satay sauce that's bursting with flavor. The satay sauce is a great staple recipe to have and can also be poured over vegetables, in a stir fry or as a sauce for noodles.

Preparation Time
10 minutes

Total Time
30 minutes

Makes
4 servings

INGREDIENTS

FOR THE TOFU SKEWERS

14oz / 400g firm tofu
2 tbsp soy sauce
2 tbsp sesame oil
1 tbsp water
1 tsp rice vinegar
1 clove garlic, crushed
1-inch ginger, peeled and grated
1 green pepper, chopped into squares
1 red pepper, chopped into squares
4-8 wooden skewers, soaked in water for at least 30 minutes

FOR THE SATAY SAUCE

1 tsp sesame oil
½ inch ginger, peeled and grated
2 medium cloves garlic, finely chopped
6 tbsp natural peanut butter
½ tbsp brown sugar
1 cup canned coconut milk
1 ½ tbsp soy sauce
1 tbsp freshly squeezed lime juice
¼ tsp chili flakes

DIRECTIONS

To start, remove tofu from packaging and press between two towels to remove excess water. You can use something weighted, such as a large saucepan or a heavy chopping board and place this on top of the tofu to squeeze out as much moisture as possible for a minimum of 10 minutes. This process will allow the tofu to absorb much more flavor. After 10 minutes chop tofu into cubes.

Once the tofu has been pressed combine soy sauce, sesame oil, water, vinegar, garlic, and ginger in a medium bowl then add tofu, gently mixing to ensure each cube is evenly coated in the marinade. Leave to marinate for 10-15 minutes or overnight if possible.

You can make the satay sauce while the tofu is marinating. Heat sesame oil in a heavy bottomed pan over medium heat and once hot add garlic and ginger, stirring constantly for a minute. Add the peanut butter, sugar, and coconut milk and stir until the peanut butter has melted. Add the soy sauce, lime juice, and chili flakes and continue to cook over low heat for 5-10 minutes until the sauce has thickened. Remove from the heat and set aside.

Preheat the grill.

Thread the pre-soaked wooden skewers with alternative pieces of tofu cubes and pepper (if you do not soak them they will burn under the grill).

Grill for 5-7 minutes, turning the skewers frequently to ensure each side is cooked and the tofu does not burn.

Serve with warm satay sauce.

CRUNCHY CASHEW COCONUT RICE WITH GINGER PEANUT DRIZZLE

Crunchy cashew nuts, creamy coconut rice and crispy vegetables make this Thai-inspired rice salad irresistible. It keeps well in the fridge and is great for a light lunch, especially with the peanut ginger drizzle.

Preparation Time
15 minutes

Total Time
30 minutes

Makes
4 servings

INGREDIENTS

FOR THE COCONUT RICE

1 cup uncooked white rice, washed thoroughly
1 (14oz / 400g) can coconut milk
1 garlic clove, minced
1 tsp salt
1 cup vegetable stock or water

FOR THE SALAD

1 red bell peppers, finely sliced
½ small red cabbage, shredded
1 cup carrots, shredded
½ red onion, finely chopped
¼ cucumber, thinly sliced
1 cup fresh cilantro, chopped
½ cup scallions, thinly sliced
½ cup unsalted cashews, finely chopped

FOR THE GINGER PEANUT SAUCE

1/3 cup peanut butter
1 tbsp brown sugar
3 tsp fresh ginger, grated
1 tbsp rice vinegar
2 tsp red wine vinegar (optional)
2 tsp sesame oil

3-4 tbsp water
1 tbsp freshly squeezed lime juice

DIRECTIONS

In a medium saucepan add coconut milk, garlic and stock, cover and bring to a boil. Once the liquid is boiling add the rice and reduce to a simmer. Cover and cook for 17 minutes, do not open the lid while cooking. Once the cooking time is up remove from the heat and leave to sit with the lid on for an additional 10 minutes.

While the rice is cooking you can prepare the peanut sauce. In a small saucepan combine peanut butter and brown sugar on a low heat until smooth. Do not allow mixture to simmer or boil. Add ginger, rice vinegar, sesame oil, and red wine vinegar (if using) and mix well. Add water and thin to required consistency then add lime juice. Set aside.

In a large serving bowl add all chopped vegetables and crushed cashew nuts. Fluff rice using a fork and add to vegetables, mixing well.

Drizzle with peanut sauce and serve warm.

QUINOA, AVOCADO & SPINACH SUSHI ROLLS

Sushi has the reputation of being difficult to make, however, this recipe is easy-to-follow and uses fresh and healthy ingredients for a delicious and filling meal.

Preparation Time
15 minutes

Total Time
35 minutes

Makes
16 sushi rolls

INGREDIENTS

1 cup uncooked quinoa, thoroughly washed
2 cups water
3 tbsp rice vinegar
1 tsp maple syrup or 1 tsp brown sugar
¼ tsp salt
½ cucumber, cut into very thin slices

1 cup loosely packed fresh spinach
1 ripe avocado, peeled, pitted and cut into thin slices
4 sheets nori sushi wrap (not with fish flavoring)
Wasabi to serve (optional)

Sushi mat for rolling

DIRECTIONS

Pour 2 cups of water in a saucepan and bring to a rolling boil. Add quinoa, reduce to a gentle simmer and cook covered for around 15-17 minutes or until all the water has been absorbed.

While the quinoa is cooking take a small bowl and combine rice vinegar, maple syrup (or sugar) and salt. Set aside.

Once the quinoa has finished cooking use a fork to fluff it up and transfer it from the saucepan to a large plate. Add the vinegar-soy mixture to the quinoa, 1 tablespoon at a time, slowly mixing so that it is well combined.

Place a nori sheet on a sushi mat and spread ¼ of the quinoa mix evenly over the entire sheet, except the last two inches as you will need to dampen this strip in order for it to stick.

Place a little spinach on top and add a few cucumber and avocado slices. Roll up very tightly, and as you come to the end dampen your fingers to wet the end strip, pressing down lightly in order to make it stick. Repeat with the remaining ingredients until you have made a total of 4 rolls.

Use a very sharp knife to cut each roll evenly into 4 sushi pieces.

Serve immediately with wasabi, or store in an airtight container in the fridge for 3 days.

SPICY SICHUAN EGGPLANT

This meal combines hot and spicy authentic flavors from the Sichuan province. The eggplants are stir fried to create a tender and silky texture and contrasts beautifully with the sweet and savory sauce.

Preparation Time
15 minutes

Total Time
30 minutes

Makes
4 servings

INGREDIENTS

2 large eggplants, cut into 1-inch cubes
1 medium onion, chopped
2 heaped tbsp fresh cilantro, chopped
2 tbsp sesame oil
2 tbsp coconut oil
6 garlic cloves, peeled and minced
3 tbsp brown sugar
4 tbsp sriracha or chili sauce

3 tbsp soy sauce
1 cup tomato sauce
1 tbsp rice vinegar
1 tbsp white vinegar
1 tbsp chili flakes
¼ tsp coarse salt
1 ½ tbsp sesame seeds
½ cup water
3 tbsp scallions, to garnish
White rice to serve

DIRECTIONS

Heat 2 tbsp sesame oil a frying pan. Once hot add the onions and saute for 3-4 minutes until soft, then add the eggplant. Add salt and the chili flakes and stir frequently. Cook for 6-8 minutes until the eggplant is tender but not mushy. Transfer to a bowl and set aside.

In the same pan heat 1 tbsp coconut oil and once hot add garlic and ginger, and saute for 2-3 minutes.

Mix in sesame seeds, tomato sauce, brown sugar, chili sauce, molasses, soy sauce, rice vinegar, white vinegar, and water.

Combine well and simmer on a low heat for 10 minutes until the sauce thickens.

Add the eggplant mixture to the sauce along with chopped cilantro and mix to incorporate all flavors, frying for around 5 minutes.

Remove from heat, garnish with scallions and serve over white rice.

MALAYSIAN LAKSA

Laksa is a spicy coconut noodle soup that is absolutely jam packed with flavor. This wonderful and authentic recipe uses fresh ingredients to make an easy laksa pasta, without needing to resort to the bottled store bought version. The laksa paste can be frozen so you could make double and keep it in the freezer for an easy dinner another night.

Preparation Time
10 minutes

Total Time
30 minutes

Makes
4 servings

INGREDIENTS

FOR THE LAKSA PASTE

3 tbsp vegetable oil
1 tbsp cilantro seeds
1 tbsp cumin seeds
3 shallots, finely chopped
3 large cloves garlic, crushed
1-inch ginger, peeled and grated
1 tbsp turmeric
2 limes, freshly squeezed
1 bird's eye chili / red Thai chili, chopped (remove seeds depending on heat preference)
1 tbsp sriracha or other chili sauce
2 large lemongrass stalks

FOR THE LAKSA BROTH

1 tsp sesame oil
3-4 tbsp Laksa paste, or more depending on heat preference
2 cups / 500ml vegetable stock
2 can (400ml each) coconut milk
3 tbsp soy sauce
4 large kaffir lime leaves
1 tbsp brown sugar
1 cup baby corn, quartered

1 large zucchini, chopped into cubes
1 large carrot, sliced
1 packet deep fried tofu puffs (found in Asian grocery stores) or 1 packet of pre-cooked tofu pieces
7oz / 200g rice noodles
3.5oz / 100g bean sprouts
½ cup fresh cilantro, roughly chopped
2 tbsp black or white sesame seeds

DIRECTIONS

Heat oil in a skillet over medium heat and once hot add cumin and cilantro seeds, moving them around constantly. Fry for a minute or until they become fragrant then add the shallots. Cook for 3-4 minutes until they have softened then add the garlic and ginger, stirring for a minute. Transfer shallot mixture to a food processor or high-speed blender along with all other laksa paste ingredients and blend until you have a fine paste.

In a large pot heat sesame oil with 3-4 tbsp laksa paste (start with 3 and add the fourth later once you have tested the heat). Pour in vegetable stock, coconut milk, soy sauce, lime leaves, and brown sugar. Slowly bring to a boil.

Once boiling reduce to a simmer and add the baby corn, zucchini, and carrot and simmer for 10 minutes until soft.

While the vegetables are softening cook the noodles according to package direction then add them to the broth.

Remove from the heat and stir in bean sprouts and cilantro. Garnish with sesame seeds and serve immediately while hot.

The laksa paste will keep in the fridge for 2 weeks or in the freezer for 3 months. The laksa soup will keep in an airtight container for 3 days and you will find it to be even tastier as the flavors marry together.

VIETNAMESE PHO

Pho is a flavorsome Vietnamese noodle soup consisting of aromatic spices, fresh herbs and vegetables. It is light yet filling, and very easy to make at home. This vegan version includes the addition of extra vegetables making it a hearty and satisfying meal.

Preparation Time
15 minutes

Total Time
45-60 minutes

Makes
4 servings

INGREDIENTS

FOR THE BROTH

10.5oz / 300g shiitake mushrooms
3 inches fresh ginger, grated
6-8 garlic cloves, peeled and minced
1 lemongrass, chopped
2 cinnamon sticks
¼ head fennel, chopped
1 medium onion, chopped
4 scallions, chopped
1/3 cup soy sauce
4 cups water
4 cups vegetable stock
1 tbsp rice wine vinegar
¼ tsp coarse salt
8oz / 230g rice noodles, cooked
Sesame oil (Can be substituted for vegetable oil)

FOR THE TOPPINGS

3.5oz / 100g bean sprouts
1 lime, cut into 8 wedges
½ head broccoli, cut into small florets and lightly steamed
2 cups Chinese greens (bok choy, Chinese broccoli etc), lightly steamed
¼ head cabbage, thinly sliced
4-5 scallions, chopped

Handful of fresh herbs - e.g mint, cilantro, basil

DIRECTIONS

In a large saucepan add sesame oil. Once hot saute onions for 3-4 minutes until soft. Add ginger and garlic and cook for 1-2 minutes until fragrant.

Stir in shiitake mushrooms and cook on medium-high for a further minute or two. Add lemongrass, cinnamon, scallions and fennel, and continually stir to mix in all flavors.

After 2-3 minutes pour in vegetable stock, water, soy sauce, rice wine vinegar and salt. Bring to a boil then reduce and allow to simmer for a minimum of 30 minutes. The longer you simmer the soup the more the flavors will infuse.

Pho is traditionally strained before serving, removing the fennel, onions, mushrooms etc, however you can leave the vegetables in for a more chunky and filling soup.

Garnish and serve with noodles and toppings.

QUICK & EASY MISO SOUP

With only 6 ingredients this Miso Soup can be on your table in 15 minutes. It's light and refreshing and makes a lovely appetizer or a filling lunch. Be sure to find Miso paste without bonito (fish flavor) as this ingredient makes it non-vegan. You can omit the nori if you have trouble finding it, however, this does add another depth of authentic flavor.

Preparation Time
5 minutes

Total Time
15 minutes

Makes
4 servings

INGREDIENTS

1 cup green chard, bok choy or other dark green leaf, chopped
1 cup scallions, chopped
½ cup firm tofu, cut into small cubes
6-8 tbsp white miso paste (fermented soybean paste)
½ cup or 2 sheets nori (dried seaweed), cut into large rectangles
8 cups water

DIRECTIONS

In a large saucepan bring water to low simmer, add nori and simmer for 6-8 minutes.

While the nori is simmering place the miso paste in a small bowl, add a few tablespoons of hot water and whisk until smooth. Stir the paste into the hot soup along with leafy greens, scallions and tofu.

Leave to cook, uncovered, on a low simmer for 10-15 minutes.

Serve hot.

The soup can be stored in the fridge in an airtight container for up to 5 days.

GYOZA (JAPANESE DUMPLINGS)

These moreish little dumplings are stuffed with juicy vegetables and are fried first so that one side is crisp and the other is softly steamed. You could make an extra portion of the filling and freeze it to cut the preparation time in half when making them again.

Preparation Time
30 minutes

Total Time
40 minutes

Makes
36 gyoza

INGREDIENTS

FOR THE FILLING

8.8oz / 250g firm tofu, chopped into very small cubes
Half small head of cabbage, grated
3.5oz / 100g mushrooms, finely chopped (you can use any variety you want)
1 medium carrot, finely chopped
1 tbsp sesame oil
3 garlic cloves, minced
1 tbsp fresh ginger, peeled and grated
2 tbsp soy sauce
1 tbsp rice wine vinegar
½ cup vegetable stock
2 tbsp cornstarch
36 gyoza papers (or wonton wrappers)

FOR THE SAUCE

4 tbsp soy sauce
3 tbsp rice vinegar
1 tbsp sesame oil
½ tsp dried chili powder if you want a spicy sauce

DIRECTIONS

FOR THE FILLING:

Heat the oil in a large frying pan and saute garlic and ginger for 1 minute until fragrant. Stir in cabbage, mushrooms, carrot and tofu. Fry for 4-5 minutes until the vegetables and tofu start to soften. Add soy sauce, rice wine vinegar and stock. Mix well to combine and allow to cook for 5-6 minutes, stirring frequently.

Add cornstarch, ½ tbsp at a time and mix well after each addition. Remove from the heat and allow to cool down for 10-15 minutes until cool enough to touch.

FOR THE GYOZA:

Have all the items ready as this will make the process much easier. You will need the filling, the gyoza wrappers and a small bowl of water to wet your fingers. Heat vegetable oil in a pan with a lid. Prepare the wrappers by laying them out in a single layer on a clean work surface while the oil is heating up.

Scoop around 1 tbsp of the mixture into your hands and use your palms roll it into a ball. Place the ball of mixture in the center of a gyoza wrapper, wet your fingertip and trace a line around the edges of half the wrapper. Now fold the wrapper in half over the filling and pinch the wrapping together using your forefinger and thumb in order to seal it.

Place all the Gyoza dumplings in the hot oil at the same time, with the seam side facing up, add a little water to cover up to 1/3 of the Gyoza. Cover the pan and cook over medium-high heat for 3-4 minutes. While the gyoza is steaming mix the sauce ingredients together using a whisk and place in a shallow bowl suitable for dipping.

Once the water has reduced to half, uncover the pan and cook until the remainder of the water has evaporated. The gyoza are done once the bottom of the dumplings have browned.

Transfer to a large serving plate along with dipping sauce.

SIDES

NASU DENGAKU
(MISO GLAZED EGGPLANT)

This classic Japanese side dish features tender eggplants with a sweet and savory sticky miso glaze and topped with sesame seeds. It's great served as a side dish or even as a main course with steamed rice.

Preparation Time
10 minutes (+ 30 minutes to salt the eggplant)

Total Time
20 minutes

Makes
4 servings

INGREDIENTS

4 small eggplants
1 tsp salt
½ cup hatcho miso or 2 tbsp white + 2 tbsp red miso mixed together
4 tbsp mirin
1 tbsp rice vinegar
1 tbsp maple syrup or sugar
2 tsp sesame oil
4 tbsp sesame seeds

DIRECTIONS

Slice the eggplants in half, lengthways, as evenly as possible. Sprinkle salt onto the inside of the eggplant and leave for 30 minutes for the salt to remove any bitterness. Rinse with cold water and pat dry, removing as much excess water as possible with a kitchen towel.

Score the eggplant diagonally in both directions (a criss-cross pattern) to create small squares using a sharp knife.

Preheat the grill. Brush the eggplant with a little sesame oil and place on a foil lined baking tray in the middle of your oven, for 10 minutes, turning over once after 5 minutes.

Remove the eggplants, brush generously with the miso glaze and place back in the oven for 3-4 minutes. Keep an eye on the eggplants as they are prone to burning.

Remove from the oven and sprinkle each half with ½ tablespoon of sesame seeds. Serve immediately while hot.

CHINESE SPECIAL FRIED RICE

The secret to this dish is to use leftover cold rice. It absorbs so much more of the flavor and gives the dish that authentic texture that you find in restaurants. If you do not have leftover rice, simply boil a batch, spread it over a large plate and leave it in the fridge for 30 minutes to cool down before cooking. The recipe also uses frozen vegetables, making this super quick and easy to whip up.

Preparation Time
5 minutes

Total Time
15 minutes

Makes
4 servings

INGREDIENTS

5 cups pre-cooked cold rice
2 tbsp sesame or vegetable oil
1 small white onion, finely chopped
3 garlic cloves, minced
1 tsp fresh ginger, grated
2 cups frozen mixed vegetables

2 cups bean sprouts
½ tsp turmeric
3 tbsp soy sauce
1 cup mushrooms, thinly sliced (you can use any variety you like)

DIRECTIONS

Heat oil in a large wok over medium-high heat. Add onions and saute for 2-3 minutes until tender, then add ginger and garlic and cook for a further minute.

Add frozen vegetables and cook until defrosted and warmed throughout, about 3-4 minutes. Stir in mushrooms and saute while frequently stirring.

Add turmeric and mix well to combine, then throw in cold rice and stir constantly to incorporate all ingredients and break up any clumps. Pour in soy sauce. Serve immediately.

JAPANESE TEMPURA

Tempura is a Japanese dish consisting of either seafood or vegetables which have been battered in a very light and crisp coating. Our appetising vegan version uses sparkling water to ensure the batter stays light and crisp.

Preparation Time
15 minutes

Total Time
15 minutes

Makes
4 servings

INGREDIENTS

4 cups vegetable, sunflower or canola cooking oil
1 ¼ cups all-purpose flour
1 tbsp cornstarch
½ tsp salt
1/3 cups ice-cold fizzy water

2-3 ice cubes
3.5oz / 100g firm vegetables, cut into bite-sized pieces (e.g. broccoli, mushroom, zucchini, sweet potato etc)

DIRECTIONS

Heat the oil in a large pot or wok until it reaches 350°c.

Make sure all the vegetables are prepped and the oil is hot before you make the batter.

Whisk together the flour, cornstarch and salt then add the carbonated water and whisk until just combined then add the ice cubes. The key to making great tempura is to not over whisk the batter, it is fine if lumps remain. You should also work fast and use the batter immediately to ensure it remains cold.

Dip the vegetables into the batter, one at a time, then carefully drop them into the oil. Do not fry too many at once as this will reduce the temperature of the oil resulting in your tempura not getting crispy. Cook each piece for 1-2 minutes, turning once to ensure they are evenly cooked.

Remove with a slotted spoon and transfer to a paper towel lined plate.

Serve immediately once all the tempura have cooked.

TOD MAN KHAO POD
(THAI CORN FRITTERS)

These fritters are oven baked instead of fried, making them much healthier yet still retaining the crisp and crunchy outer coating. There are very few steps involved in this recipe and it only takes 10 minutes to prepare.

Preparation Time
10 minutes

Total Time
40 minutes

Makes
6-8 litres

INGREDIENTS

2 cups corn, frozen or canned
¾ cup all-purpose flour
¼ cup cornstarch
¾ tsp baking powder
3 scallions, thinly sliced
1/3 cup cilantro, chopped
1 tsp lime zest

1 ½ tbsp soy sauce
1 ½ tbsp red curry paste
¼ tsp red chili flakes
1 lb / 450g silken tofu
½ cup water
1 tbsp vegetable or canola oil

DIRECTIONS

Place tofu in a food processor or blender and pulse until it has become smooth. Set aside.

Preheat the oven to 170°c. Grease a baking tray with a little oil or line with parchment paper.

In a large bowl combine mashed tofu, corn, flour, cornstarch, baking powder, scallions, cilantro, lime zest, soy sauce, red curry paste, chili flakes and water. Mix well until a thick batter has formed and all ingredients are thoroughly mixed together.

Use a large spoon or ice cream scoop to mould batter into a round shape and flatten a little with your hands or using the back of a spoon to form a fritter. Place on the baking tray and repeat with remaining batter.

Bake for 27-30 minutes until edges have browned. Flip fritter over after 15 minutes of cooking.

Serve immediately while hot and crispy.

CRUNCHY ASIAN SALAD WITH SWEET SESAME VINAIGRETTE

This vibrant, colorful and delicious salad is an Asian twist on a classic recipe which replaces rice with quinoa. It's loaded with veggies and is bursting with flavor from the addition of the Asian Vinaigrette.

Preparation Time
10 minutes

Total Time
30 minutes

Makes
4 servings

INGREDIENTS

FOR THE SALAD

4 cups red cabbage, shredded
1 cup uncooked quinoa
2 cups water
2 cups carrots, shredded
1 red bell pepper, thinly sliced
½ cup scallions, thinly sliced
½ cup unsalted cashew nuts, lightly toasted and roughly chopped

FOR THE SWEET SESAME VINAIGRETTE

1/3 cup vegetable or olive oil
3 tbsp rice wine vinegar
1 tbsp agave, maple syrup or brown sugar
2 tsp soy sauce
1 tsp sesame oil
1 tsp freshly squeezed lemon or lime juice
2 tbsp sesame seeds
Pinch of coarse salt
Pinch of black pepper

DIRECTIONS

Bring 2 cups water to a rolling boil then add quinoa. Reduce to a gentle simmer and cook covered for 17-20 minutes or according to packet directions. Once cooked remove from heat and fluff up using a fork.

In a large serving bowl add all coleslaw ingredients together and toss until well combined.

To make the vinaigrette whisk all ingredients together.

Drizzle vinaigrette over salad and serve.

The salad will keep in an airtight container in the fridge for 2 days.

CHILI GARLIC MUSHROOMS

This easy side dish combines exotic flavors with a spicy kick. Stir-frying enables the mushrooms to be cooked to perfection and makes this a quick and easy dish using ingredients you are likely to already have in your cupboard.

Preparation Time
5 minutes

Total Time
10 minutes

Makes
4 servings

INGREDIENTS

8.8oz / 250g button mushrooms, washed and patted dry
3 tbsp olive oil
5 garlic cloves, minced
½ cup parsley, finely chopped
1 medium red chili, finely chopped (you can use fresh or dried)
2 tbsp freshly squeezed lemon juice
4 tbsp dry sherry
2 tsp soy sauce
Pinch of salt and pepper to taste

DIRECTIONS

Heat oil in a frying pan or wok over medium-high heat. Once hot add garlic and saute for 30 seconds. Add mushrooms, parsley, chili, lemon juice, sherry and soy sauce.

Stir-fry for 5-6 minutes until the mushrooms are cooked throughout. Stir constantly to prevent the mushrooms from burning. If the mixture is sticking to the bottom of the pan add a splash of water.

Season with salt and pepper and serve immediately while hot.

SAUTÉED BROCCOLI WITH ASIAN GARLIC SAUCE

Fragrant garlic and crispy broccoli make this dish a favorite for take-aways and in restaurants. You can easily recreate this tasty traditional dish in your own kitchen and it won't take you more than 10 minutes.

Preparation Time
5 minutes

Total Time
10 minutes

Makes
4 servings

INGREDIENTS

2 tbsp sesame oil
1 large broccoli head, chopped into small florets
3 garlic cloves, minced
1 tsp fresh ginger, peeled and grated
2 tbsp soy sauce
½ cup vegetable stock
1 tbsp cornstarch mixed with 2 tbsp water
½ - 1 tsp dried chili flakes

DIRECTIONS

In a small bowl whisk together garlic, ginger and soy sauce.

Heat oil in a wok or frying pan over medium-high heat and add broccoli. Stir-fry for 3-4 minutes, stirring constantly to prevent the florets from sticking to the bottom of the pan.

Reduce heat to medium-low and pour in soy sauce and cornstarch mixture, stirring well to coat all of the broccoli. Keep stirring for about 3 minutes for the sauce to thicken. Taste and season with salt and pepper if required.

Remove from heat and serve immediately while hot.

SOFT CHINESE BAO BUNS

A baozi (bao bun) is a fluffy steamed bun with a soy bean paste filling that is very popular in Asian cuisine. The bun is delicate and light with a delicious center, that can be eaten as a snack or served as a side dish to accompany a main meal.

Preparation Time
30 minutes

Total Time
1 hour 30 minutes
(incl. 1 hour for dough to rest)

Makes
4 servings

INGREDIENTS

FOR THE DOUGH

10.5oz / 300g all-purpose flour
1 packet instant yeast or 2¼ tsp
1 cup warm water
1 tbsp oil for brushing

FOR THE FILLING

14oz / 400g firm tofu, drained, pressed and cut into very small cubes

3 scallions, chopped
1 tsp chili bean paste or soybean paste (found in the Asian section of large supermarkets)
1 large garlic clove, chopped
1-inch fresh ginger, grated
1 tsp sesame or vegetable oil
1 tsp coarse salt
2 tsp soy sauce

DIRECTIONS

In a small bowl add warm water (if you have a cooking thermometer the water needs to be 35°c) and gently stir in the yeast. Set aside for 5 minutes. You should see small bubbles forming at the surface.

In a large bowl add the flour then slowly pour in the water-yeast mixture, stirring with a wooden spoon.

On a clean, lightly floured surface knead the dough with your hands for 5-6 minutes. It may be a little sticky at first but continue to dust the surface with a little flour at a time and it should start coming together. Place in a large bowl, cover with a cloth and leave to rest in a dry area for 1 hour or until the dough doubles in size.

After an hour transfer to a lightly floured surface again and punch the air out by pushing your fist into the center of the dough, pulling it back into a ball shape and repeating a few times.

Roll the dough out into a long log of around 1-inch in diameter and using a knife cut the log into small pieces of around 1-inch long. Flatten these with your hands or by pressing them with the back of a cup to form a thin round 'coin'. These are called baozi and are to be used as wrappers. Keep in mind they need to be large enough to fill with stuffing. Set aside in a single layer on a large plate or your kitchen work surface while you prepare the filling.

Heat oil in a wok or pan over medium-high heat, and once hot add ginger, garlic and bean paste, stirring constantly for 1 minute until fragrant.

Add tofu, salt, and soy sauce and mix well. Stir-fry for a further 5-7 minutes until the tofu is cooked. Add scallions then remove from the heat.

Prepare your steamer.

Place one heaped tablespoon of the filling into the center of the baozi and begin to fold the edges clockwise, pinching the wrapper as you go along. Move your thumb and forefinger around in a clockwise direction, pinching the wrapper together until the bun is sealed.

Lightly brush the bun with some oil on the top and bottom and place in the steamer. Repeat with remaining wrappers and filling.

Steam buns for 15 minutes. Serve immediately while warm.

COCONUT & LIME RICE

Coriander, coconut, and lime transform plain rice into a delicately flavored and exotic side dish, perfect to accompany a curry or main meal.

Preparation Time
5 minutes

Total Time
25 minutes

Makes
4 servings

INGREDIENTS

1 ½ cup jasmine rice, washed thoroughly
1 ½ cup canned coconut milk
1 ½ cup water
1 lime, zested
2 tsp freshly squeezed lime juice
2 tbsp fresh cilantro, chopped
½ tsp coarse salt
½ tsp black pepper

DIRECTIONS

In a large saucepan bring salt, pepper, coconut milk and water to a boil then add the rice. Stir to combine and release any grains that have stuck to the bottom of the saucepan then reduce heat to a low simmer and cook covered for 14-17 minutes.

Remove from the heat and stir in lime zest, lime juice and cilantro. Use a fork to fluff the rice up.

Serve immediately while piping hot.

COCONUT CRUSTED TOFU BITES WITH CREAMY THAI GREEN SAUCE

This tasty bite-sized finger food can be served as an appetizer or as a side dish. The sweet crusty coating is made with shredded coconut and cashew nuts, and the bites are then dipped into a beautifully creamy and exotically flavored sauce.

Preparation Time
20 minutes

Total Time
1 hour and 10 minutes

Makes
18-24 bites

INGREDIENTS

FOR THE GREEN CURRY SAUCE

½ cup full-fat coconut milk, canned
½ - ¾ tsp green curry paste
2 tbsp pineapple juice
1 tsp finely grated lime zest
1 tsp brown sugar
¾ tsp arrowroot powder or cornstarch

FOR THE COCONUT TOFU BITES

2 tsp Dijon mustard
¼ cup full-fat coconut milk, canned
2 tbsp freshly squeezed lime juice
1 tsp brown sugar
¼ tsp coarse salt
1.1 lb / 500g firm tofu
1 cup desiccated coconut
¼ cup unsalted cashew nuts, crushed

DIRECTIONS

To start, remove tofu from packaging and press between two towels to remove excess water. You can use something weighted, such as a large saucepan or chopping board and place this on top of the tofu to squeeze out as much moisture as possible for a minimum of 10 minutes. This process will allow the tofu to absorb much more flavor. After 10 minutes chop tofu into small bite-size cubes.

FOR THE DIPPING SAUCE:

While the tofu is being pressed make the sauce. In a small saucepan combine coconut milk, green curry paste, pineapple juice, brown sugar, and lime zest over medium-low heat. Once the liquid starts to simmer remove 2 tbsp and transfer into a small bowl. Whisk in cornstarch or arrowroot powder until a smooth paste is formed then pour back into coconut milk mixture. Stir frequently while the sauce thickens, around 4-7 minutes.

Remove from the heat, transfer to a small serving bowl and allow to cool to room temperature. This sauce can be made up to one day ahead, covered in plastic wrap and left in the fridge overnight.

FOR THE COCONUT TOFU BITES:

Preheat the oven to 190°c. Line a baking tray with parchment paper and spray with nonstick spray or grease with a little coconut oil.

In a medium bowl whisk mustard, coconut milk, lime, sugar, and salt until well combined. Place cubed tofu in the mixture and use a spatula to ensure each piece is coated. Leave to soak up the flavor for a minimum of 10 minutes.

In a shallow dish or large plate pour in the desiccated coconut and cashew nuts and mix well. Dip each tofu piece into the coconut-cashew mix and roll around to evenly coat each side. Make sure to allow any excess coconut-mustard mix to drip off before coating to prevent the desiccated coconut from becoming a sticky mess.

Place each coconut crusted piece on the baking tray and repeat with remaining tofu. Bake for 25-30 minutes, turning once after 15 minutes, until golden brown.

Serve immediately or allow to cool to room temperature.

DESSERTS

COCONUT MATCHA TARTS

Finally, a dessert that's healthy! The crust is made from oats, coconut, and buckwheat flour, and the smooth and creamy filling features raw cashew nuts, coconut cream, and super healthy matcha. The addition of matcha powder gives the filling a wonderfully vibrant green color.

Preparation Time
20 minutes
(+ 4 hours for cashews to soak)

Total Time
1 hour

Makes
4 mini tarts

INGREDIENTS

FOR THE CRUST

1 cup oats
½ cup desiccated coconut
1 cup buckwheat flour
¼ tsp salt
8 tsp cornstarch
4 tbsp cacao powder
6 tbsp coconut oil + 1 tsp, melted
6 tbsp maple syrup

FOR THE FILLING

1 cup raw cashews, soaked for a minimum of 4 hours or preferably overnight
2 cups / 480ml full-fat coconut cream*
4 tsp matcha powder
½ cup maple syrup
1 ½ tsp vanilla essence
3 tbsp desiccated coconut
Pinch of salt
3 tsp agar flakes + ½ cup water

* FOR THE COCONUT CREAM: This should either be the variety you can buy in a hard block or you can take a can of full-fat coconut milk, place it in the fridge overnight and use the hard cream that will have formed at the top.

DIRECTIONS

FOR THE CRUST:

Preheat the oven to 350° F. Line the base of 4 ramekins (around 4.5 inches in diameter) with parchment paper and grease the edges with around 1 teaspoon of coconut oil and set aside.

Place oats and coconut in a food processor or high-speed blender and pulse until it becomes a fine powder. Transfer to a large bowl.

Add buckwheat, salt, cornstarch and cocoa and mix well. Slowly add the coconut oil and rub the mixture in between your fingers until the flour and oil has fully combined. Add maple syrup and mix with a wooden spoon until the dough starts to come together. Cover loosely with plastic wrap and leave the dough to rest for 10 minutes.

Once the dough has rested, evenly divided it into four and press into each ramekin so that the crust evenly covers the base and the sides. Bake in the oven, on the middle shelf, for 15 minutes. Remove from the oven and cool down as the filling cannot be added when the crust is still hot.

FOR THE FILLING:

Place the agar flakes in a small saucepan with ½ cup of water and bring to a boil then lower to a simmer. Simmer for 15 minutes, stirring frequently, until the flakes have dissolved as much as possible. Remove from the heat and allow to cool down for 5 minutes or so.

While the agar agar is cooling down place drained cashews, coconut cream, matcha, maple syrup, and vanilla into a blender and pulse until smooth, scraping down the sides a few times, then add the agar agar and pulse again a few times until the mixture is completely smooth. Add the desiccated coconut and pulse once or twice to incorporate it into the mixture.

Evenly pour the filling into the four ramekins and smooth over the top with the back of a spoon.

Set the tart aside to set for 30-40 minutes then serve.

JIAN DUI (FRIED SESAME BALLS)

These sweet fried balls are commonly served as Dim Sum, and consist of a soft dough made from rice flour which is filled with red bean paste then covered in sesame seeds and finally deep fried to crispy perfection. You'll be surprised how easy this authentic recipe is to create in your very own kitchen!

Preparation Time
20 minutes

Total Time
35 minutes

Makes
8 sesame balls

INGREDIENTS

¾ cup glutinous rice flour, sieved
2 heaped tbsp sugar
1/3 cup water, boiling
Pinch of salt
1 tsp baking powder
1 tbsp vegetable oil

3.5oz / 100g sweetened red bean paste or lotus paste
¼ cup white sesame seeds
1 ½ cups vegetable oil, for frying

DIRECTIONS

In a medium bowl mix rice flour, sugar, and salt together. Add boiling water and mix well until you have a rough dough, then add vegetable oil.

Transfer to a kitchen surface lightly dusted with glutinous rice flour and knead for a few minutes until the oil has completely absorbed.

Roll the dough out into a thin 'log' and cut it into 8 equal pieces. Roll each ball out into a 'disk' then spoon ½-1 teaspoon of the red bean paste into the middle. Seal completely - ensuring there are no gaps for the red bean paste to leak then shape into a round ball.

Heat vegetable oil in a wok over medium heat. It needs to reach around 210-250°c.

Prepare two bowls, one with water and one with sesame seeds. Quickly dip each ball into the water to lightly coat it, then dip it in the sesame seeds and gently roll it in between the palms of your hands to ensure the sesame seeds stick. Continue with remaining balls.

Carefully place balls into the hot oil (you may need to do this in batches to not overcrowd the pan) and slowly deep fry for 5 minutes, without touching or moving the balls as the sesame seeds may drop off. After 5 minutes gently turn the balls over using a metal tong.

The balls will initially stay at the bottom of the pan, then slowly float to the surface of the oil. Once they start to float use the metal tongs or a pair of chopsticks to continuously submerge the balls in the hot oil and gently press them against the sides of the wok. You will see the balls expanding in size once you start to press them against the sides. Try to press each ball evenly on each side to ensure you are left with a round shape.

Once the balls have expanded to around 3 times the size they were originally and they have browned a little you can remove them from the heat using a slotted spoon and transfer to a paper towel lined plate.

Allow to cool a little but serve while warm and crisp.

It is recommended that sesame balls are eaten on they day they are made as they do not keep particularly well the following day.

COCONUT STICKY RICE WITH MANGO

Whip up a homemade version of an authentic Thai dish that is simple and easy to prepare. Creamy and rich rice is delicately flavored with sweet coconut and topped with fresh mangos. This is an indulgent dessert that is sure to be a real crowd pleaser.

Preparation Time
2 hours and 15 minutes (incl. soaking time for rice)

Total Time
45 minutes

Makes
4 mini tarts

INGREDIENTS

2 cup sticky rice, washed and soaked in water for a minimum of 2 hours (preferably overnight)
2 cup coconut milk (canned)
½ cup water or slightly more if needed
2 large mangos, peeled and cubed
3 tbsp brown sugar
⅛ tsp coarse salt
Roasted black sesame seeds to garnish (optional)

DIRECTIONS

Once the sticky rice has soaked drain the water and lay it out on a large cloth or towel, patting it dry to remove excess moisture.

Place the rice into a steamer and steam for 15 minutes.

While the rice is steaming heat the coconut milk in a small saucepan and add sugar, and salt. Keep the heat low and do not allow it to boil. Once the sugar has dissolved and the milk has thickened a little, around 5-6 minutes, remove from the heat. Transfer ½ cup of the milk to a small bowl and set aside. Pour 1 ½ cups of the coconut milk over the sticky rice and continue to steam for a further 10-15 minutes.

Once rice is cooked remove from the steamer and place on a serving plate or bowl. Allow to cool for 10 minutes before pouring the remaining ½ cup of coconut milk over the rice and laying the mango cubes over the top.

Garnish with roasted black sesame seeds if using, and serve immediately.

CRISPY BANANA FRITTERS WITH SESAME SEEDS

These fritters feature crispy and crunchy golden batter on the outside with sweet and soft banana on the inside. The secret to perfecting these fritters is to get the temperature of the oil just right. You must make sure the oil is hot enough while they are frying or else they will become greasy and soggy.

Preparation Time
5 minutes

Total Time
20 minutes

Makes
5 servings

INGREDIENTS

5 bananas, cut diagonally into bite-sized chunks (4-5 pieces per banana)
Vegetable oil for frying
2 heaped tbsp desiccated coconut (optional)
3.8oz / 110g all-purpose flour or rice flour
3.5oz / 100g corn starch
4 tbsp sesame seeds
¼ tsp coarse salt
2 ½ tbsp white sugar
1 cup water
Icing sugar for dusting

DIRECTIONS

Heat the oil in a large pan or wok (1½ - 2 inches) until very hot. If you have a cooking thermometer heat the oil to 180°C, otherwise place a small piece of bread in the oil and if it turns golden brown within 30 seconds the oil is ready.

While the oil is heating mix desiccated coconut, both flours, sesame seeds, salt, sugar, and water together with a whisk until a smooth and thick batter is formed.

Dip each banana piece into the batter to evenly coat and carefully place in hot oil. Fry fritters in batches for around 3-4 minutes or until golden brown, being careful not to overcrowd the pan.

Using a slotted spoon remove each banana fritter and place on a kitchen-towel lined plate. Repeat with remaining battered banana pieces.

Dust with icing sugar and serve immediately while hot.

HUP TUL WOO
(CHINESE SWEET WALNUT SOUP)

This rich and creamy dessert has been enjoyed by the Chinese for centuries. It features walnuts, rice, and coconut milk to create something in between a porridge and a rice pudding. It is traditionally served warm, making it wonderfully comforting.

Preparation Time
10 minutes (+ 2 ½ hours for the rice to soak)

Total Time
30 minutes

Makes
4 servings

INGREDIENTS

2 cups raw walnuts + 2 tbsp to garnish
3 tbs Arborio or Carnaroli rice
1 cup boiling water
½ cup Chinese brown sugar (or use raw / brown sugar)
¼ tsp salt
1 (400ml / 15oz) can coconut milk

DIRECTIONS

Place the rice in a bowl and pour in boiling water. Cover the bowl with a plate or plastic wrap and allow the rice to soak for 2 ½ hours.

Preheat the oven to 350°F.

Line a baking tray with parchment paper and spread walnuts in a single layer. Roast for 10-12 minutes until they have slightly browned and are fragrant. Remove from the oven and transfer to a plate to cool for 5 minutes.

Drain the rice and pour into a food processor along with the walnuts and 4 cups of water. Pulse until smooth then transfer to a saucepan.

Heat the rice-walnut mixture over medium-low heat then add sugar and salt. Simmer for 15 minutes.

Pour the mixture through a sieve and into another saucepan and add coconut milk. Heat for 5 minutes then spoon into 4 bowls and garnish each bowl with a few walnuts.

GINGER-INFUSED JAPANESE RICE PUDDING

Luscious and creamy, this Japanese inspired recipe incorporates a delicate ginger flavor without it being too overpowering. The type of rice you use is important and short grain is deemed the best for absorbing the flavorsome milk and producing a silky smooth texture.

Preparation Time
15 minutes

Total Time
1 hour and 30 minutes

Makes
5 servings

INGREDIENTS

¼ cup water
1/3 cup packed brown sugar
¼ cup granulated sugar
1 ½ tbsp fresh ginger, peeled and grated
2 cups almond milk

1 ½ cups soy milk
¾ cup short-grain rice, washed
6-7 fresh strawberries, sliced
Crystallised ginger for garnish (optional)

DIRECTIONS

In a small saucepan heat water, white sugar, and brown sugar over medium-low heat. Bring to a boil then reduce the heat to a low simmer. Leave the syrup to simmer for 25 minutes, stirring occasionally.

Meanwhile, place ginger in a cheesecloth and securely tie with a piece of string. Heat a saucepan over low heat and combine almond milk, soy milk, and the ginger. Bring to a gentle simmer, cooking for around 20 minutes and stirring occasionally.

Remove the bag of ginger and discard. Stir in rice and syrup and bring mixture to a boil.

Reduce heat to medium and allow mixture to simmer, uncovered, for 30 minutes until the pudding thickens and the rice is tender.

Remove from heat, serve in bowls and top with sliced strawberries and crystallized ginger.

BLACK SESAME SEED ICE CREAM

Black sesame seeds are popular throughout Asia and are included in many savoury dishes. This unique recipe utilises their wonderfully nutty flavor and brilliant black color in a sweet ice cream dessert. This ice cream is creamy, rich and delicious - and best of all can be made without an ice cream maker.

Preparation Time
15 minutes

Total Time
3 hours

Makes
8 servings

INGREDIENTS

1/3 cup black sesame seeds
2 ½ tbsp maple syrup
1 can (14oz / 400ml) full-fat coconut milk
1½ cups unsweetened dairy free milk

3.5oz / 100g raw sugar or coconut sugar
⅛ tsp salt
1 tsp vanilla extract
3 tbsp cornflour

DIRECTIONS

Place the black sesame seeds on a dry frying pan over medium heat and roast until they start to become fragrant and pop. Remove from the heat and transfer to a small bowl to cool for a few minutes. Pour the seeds into a food processor, high-speed blender or coffee grinder and blend until they have become a fine powder. Transfer to a small bowl and combine with maple syrup to form a thick paste.

Place a saucepan over medium heat and pour in 1 can of coconut milk, sugar and salt, and whisk until the sugar has dissolved.

In a medium bowl pour in the dairy free milk and whisk in the cornflour until completely smooth and no lumps remain. Add this mixture to the coconut milk and increase the heat to medium high, whisking constantly to ensure no lumps form for around 5 minutes or until the mixture thickens.

Remove from the heat, transfer to a large bowl and stir in the sesame seed paste and vanilla essence until fully combined. Cover the surface with plastic wrap to prevent a skin from forming and place in the fridge to chill for a minimum of 2 hours.

Churn in an ice cream maker according to machine instructions. If you do not have an ice cream maker you can pour the mixture into a flat metal tray, cover and chill in the freezer. After 40 minutes give the mixture a good mash with a fork to break down the ice crystals, and do this twice again after each 40 minute interval. If you want your ice cream to be really smooth you could place the mixture in a food processor instead of mashing with a fork.

Remove the ice cream 15 minutes before you are ready to serve for it to soften a little.

The ice cream will keep for 3 months in an airtight container in the freezer.

WATERMELON & COCONUT ICE CREAM

This exotic and indulgent ice cream is sugar-free and takes only 10 minutes to prepare. Refreshing and light, it can be eaten guilt free and is the perfect snack to curb a sweet tooth.

Preparation Time
10 minutes

Total Time
3 hours and 30 minutes

Makes
4 servings

INGREDIENTS

1 can full-fat coconut milk
4 large Medjool dates, pitted
1 tsp vanilla extract
1½ cups watermelon, seeds removed and cubed

DIRECTIONS

Line a bread tin or cake pan with plastic wrap and set aside.

Add all ingredients to a blender and pulse until smooth and fully combined.

Pour mixture into lined tin and cover top loosely with plastic wrap, then freeze for 3 hours.

After 3 hours remove from the tin and leave to thaw for 10 minutes at room temperature.

Using a knife, break the ice-cream into smaller chunks and place back into the blender. It will need to be blended one more time in order to achieve a smooth and creamy texture. Pulse again for 2-3 minutes, then pour back into the lined tin.

Freeze for 30 minutes then serve. Keep ice cream covered with plastic wrap while in the freezer and it will keep for up to 3 months.

SWEET THAI COCONUT PANCAKES

These sweet little pancakes are a common street food in Thailand and will take you to coconut heaven. They are light and fluffy with a crispy golden coating making them not too heavy after a big meal.

Preparation Time
5 minutes

Total Time
15 minutes

Makes
6-8 fritters

INGREDIENTS

2 ½ cups desiccated coconut
½ cup all-purpose flour
¼ cup cornflour
½ cup water
1 tsp vanilla extract
2 tbsp granulated sugar

DIRECTIONS

Add all ingredients to a large bowl and whisk together until fully combined. Add 1 tablespoon more water at a time if the batter seems a little dry.

Heat a frying pan with vegetable oil over medium-high heat. Once hot cook fritters in small batches by spooning 1 heaped tbsp of batter into the oil, flattening slightly with a spatula by gently pressing down to form the shape of a fritter, and fry on one side for 2-3 minutes, then flip over and cook on the other side for a further 2-3 minutes until golden brown and crispy.

Remove and place on a paper towel lined plate while you fry the remaining fritters.

Serve immediately while hot and crispy.

EXTRAS

SWEET CHILI DIPPING SAUCE

This versatile sauce can be used in so many ways. If you are starved for time you could even drizzle the sauce on noodles for a quick and easy dinner, or use it to add a burst of flavor to spring rolls, sesame crackers or fries.

Preparation Time
5 minutes

Total Time
5 minutes

Makes
1 cup

INGREDIENTS

4 tbsp soy sauce
4 tbsp rice vinegar
2 tbsp brown sugar
2 tbsp warm water
1 garlic clove, minced
¼ tsp red pepper flakes
1 tsp cilantro, chopped

DIRECTIONS

Add all ingredients to a bowl and whisk until well combined and the sugar has dissolved.

Store in the fridge in an airtight container for 5-7 days.

VEGAN OYSTER SAUCE

A staple in any Asian kitchen, oyster sauce is commonly used in stir fries, dips, or to flavor soups. This vegan version uses miso paste to replicate the umami flavor of oyster sauce and acts as an excellent vegan substitute.

Preparation Time
5 minutes

Total Time
5 minutes

Makes approx.
¾ cup sauce

INGREDIENTS

2 vegetable stock cube
1 cup / 240ml boiling water
4 tbsp brown miso paste
2 heaped tsp cornflour dissolved in 2 tbsp water
2 tbsp agave or maple syrup
1 tbsp soy sauce

DIRECTIONS

Heat 1 cup of water in a saucepan until it comes to a boil then add the stock cube and the miso and stir until it dissolves.

Reduce the heat to a vigorous simmer then add the cornflour-water mixture, stirring until it has thickened.

Add the maple syrup and soy sauce and continue to simmer until everything has thickened.

Remove from the heat and transfer to a jar. Allow the oyster sauce to cool down to room temperature then store, sealed, in the fridge for up to 2 weeks.

PEANUT SATAY SAUCE

Peanut satay makes a great dipping sauce, is great drizzled on a salad or can even be used to marinate tofu. It's quick and easy to make and can be made with ingredients you would commonly have in the pantry.

Preparation Time
5 minutes

Total Time
15 minutes

Makes approx.
4 servings

INGREDIENTS

1 tbsp peanut butter
1 tsp ginger, peeled and grated
2 tbsp sesame oil
2 tbsp soy sauce
1 tbsp brown sugar
1 tsp sesame seeds

DIRECTIONS

Combine all ingredients except the sesame seeds, and heat in a saucepan over medium-low. Heat until ingredients have melted together and become smooth and creamy but do not bring to a boil.

Once cooked, remove from heat and add sesame seeds. Pour over noodles or use as a dipping sauce.

Store in the fridge in an airtight container for up to 5 days.

SPINACH AND SESAME CRACKERS

The spinach in this recipe is used to bring a vibrant green color to these crackers without overpowering the flavor. The crackers have a sweet nutty taste, thanks to the sesame seeds and are perfect when dipped in sweet chili sauce or peanut satay sauce.

Preparation Time
15 minutes

Total Time
35 minutes

Makes
1 small bowl of crackers

INGREDIENTS

7oz / 200g all-purpose flour
1½ tsp baking powder
1 tsp coarse salt
½ tsp freshly ground black pepper
2 tbsp sesame seeds

1 tbsp sesame or vegetable oil
¼ cup water
2 loosely packed cups fresh spinach, washed and patted dry

DIRECTIONS

Preheat the oven to 200°C. Line a baking tray with parchment paper.

Add spinach to a blender or food processor with ¼ cup water and pulse until completely smooth. Set aside.

In a large bowl add flour, baking powder, salt, pepper and sesame seeds and mix to combine. Stir in the spinach-water mixture along with sesame oil and knead with your hands until you have formed a smooth dough. Add a little more flour if the dough is too sticky, or a tablespoon more water if it seems to dry.

On a clean and lightly floured surface roll the dough out into a thin long rectangular shape. Cut into evenly sized bite-sized squares (going across and down - length and width wise) using a sharp knife or pizza cutter. Transfer to the baking tray.

Bake for 20 minutes or until the edges have browned.

Store in an airtight container at room temperature for up to 1 week.

EDAMAME PÂTÉ

An earthy and fresh pâté made with edamame, mint, and lime juice. Perfect as a spread for crackers and wraps, or you could even add a little water and use it as a dip for sushi or chips.

Preparation Time
10 minutes

Total Time
10 minutes

Makes approx.
4 servings

INGREDIENTS

300g / 10.5oz frozen edamame
2 tbsp lime juice
1 tbsp fresh mint leaves
½ tsp salt
½ tsp pepper
Pinch of chili flakes

DIRECTIONS

Place edamame in a saucepan, pour in enough water to fully submerge them then bring to a boil. Reduce and simmer for 5 minutes until they are soft. Drain well and transfer to a food processor.

Add all other ingredients to the food processor and blend until you have a smooth paste.

Keep in an airtight container for 3-4 days.

THAI MANGO-COCONUT BUBBLE TEA

Bubble tea, also known as pearl milk tea, is a Taiwanese drink that has gained popularity over the last few years. Tapioca pearls can be found in any Asian shop or the international section of a large supermarket. This uniquely flavored sweet tea is very easy to make at home and you can experiment with various flavors.

Preparation Time
10 minutes

Total Time
50 minutes
(including chilling time)

Makes approx.
2 servings

INGREDIENTS

1 package tapioca pearls for bubble tea (found in the Asian section of large supermarkets)
2 regular black tea bags
2 cups water
1 tbsp granulated sugar

1 ripe mango, cut into small cubes
2 tbsp maple syrup or 2 tbsp brown sugar
1 can coconut milk
Crushed ice or ice cubes
Bubble tea straws (optional)

DIRECTIONS

Make 2-3 cups of strong tea. Place the pot of tea in the refrigerator to cool and steep for around 15-20 minutes.

In a small saucepan bring 2 cups of water to a boil. Add 1 tbsp sugar and tapioca pearls, reduce to a low simmer and cook for 15 minutes or according to packet directions. Drain water, transfer pearls to a small bowl and refrigerate for 20-30 minutes or until chilled.

In a cocktail shaker pour in tea, coconut milk, maple syrup and ice and shake vigorously for a minute or two.

Place tapioca pearls and mango in a glass and pour over coconut milk mixture.

Serve cold.

MORE GREAT TITLES

HIGH CEDAR PRESS

CHECK OUT THE FULL COLLECTION!

CPSIA information can be obtained
at www.ICGtesting.com
Printed in the USA
LVHW050507250122
709254LV00017B/2296